# 50 Vegan Curry Recipes for Home

By: Kelly Johnson

# Table of Contents

- Homemade Trail Mix (nuts, seeds, dried fruit)
- Apple Slices with Almond Butter
- Veggie Sticks with Hummus
- Greek Yogurt Parfait with Berries and Granola
- Roasted Chickpeas with Seasonings
- Banana Oatmeal Muffins
- Rice Cakes with Avocado and Tomato Slices
- Popcorn (lightly salted or flavored with nutritional yeast)
- Edamame (steamed and lightly salted)
- Cottage Cheese with Pineapple Chunks
- Whole Grain Crackers with Sliced Cheese
- Fruit Kabobs (skewered mixed fruit)
- Almond Energy Balls
- Quinoa Salad Cups
- Baked Sweet Potato Fries
- Cucumber Slices with Tzatziki Sauce
- Chia Seed Pudding with Mixed Berries
- Mixed Nuts (unsalted)
- Whole Grain Toast with Mashed Avocado
- Greek Yogurt Dip with Pretzel Sticks
- Carrot Cake Energy Bites
- Seaweed Snacks
- Whole Grain Pita Chips with Hummus
- Frozen Grapes
- Mini Caprese Skewers (cherry tomatoes, mozzarella, basil)
- Kale Chips
- Whole Grain Banana Bread
- Bell Pepper Slices with Guacamole
- Homemade Fruit Leather
- Almond Butter Rice Cake Sandwiches
- Berry Smoothie Popsicles
- Celery Sticks with Peanut Butter and Raisins
- Spinach and Feta Mini Frittatas
- Avocado Toast with Radish Slices
- Granola Bars (homemade with oats, nuts, and dried fruit)
- Roasted Seaweed Snacks

- Cottage Cheese with Sliced Peaches
- Veggie Sushi Rolls
- Pumpkin Seeds (roasted with cinnamon)
- Mini Whole Wheat Bagels with Cream Cheese and Tomato
- Blueberry Oatmeal Cookies
- Ants on a Log (celery sticks with peanut butter and raisins)
- Cherry Tomato and Mozzarella Skewers
- Whole Grain Crackers with Tuna Salad
- Mango Chia Seed Pudding
- Spinach and Cheese Quesadillas (whole grain tortillas)
- Roasted Red Pepper Hummus with Pita Bread
- Zucchini Chips
- Pineapple Coconut Energy Bites
- Whole Grain Muffins with Mixed Berries

**Homemade Trail Mix (nuts, seeds, dried fruit)**

Ingredients:

- 1 cup almonds
- 1 cup walnuts
- 1 cup cashews
- 1 cup pumpkin seeds
- 1 cup sunflower seeds
- 1 cup dried cranberries
- 1 cup dried apricots, chopped
- 1 cup dried mango, chopped
- 1 cup dark chocolate chips (optional)
- 1 teaspoon sea salt

Instructions:

1. Preheat your oven to 325°F (160°C).
2. Spread almonds, walnuts, cashews, pumpkin seeds, and sunflower seeds evenly on a baking sheet lined with parchment paper.
3. Roast the nuts and seeds in the preheated oven for 10-12 minutes, or until lightly golden brown and fragrant. Make sure to stir halfway through to ensure even roasting.
4. Remove the baking sheet from the oven and let the nuts and seeds cool completely.
5. Once cooled, transfer the roasted nuts and seeds to a large mixing bowl.
6. Add dried cranberries, chopped apricots, chopped mango, and dark chocolate chips (if using) to the bowl.
7. Sprinkle the sea salt over the mixture.
8. Gently toss everything together until well combined.
9. Transfer the trail mix to an airtight container or portion into individual snack bags for easy grab-and-go snacks.
10. Enjoy your homemade trail mix as a nutritious and satisfying snack at school, work, or on your outdoor adventures!

**Apple Slices with Almond Butter**

Ingredients:

- 2 apples (any variety you prefer)
- 1/4 cup almond butter
- 1 tablespoon honey or maple syrup (optional)
- 1 teaspoon cinnamon (optional)
- Squeeze of lemon juice (optional, to prevent browning)

Instructions:

1. Wash the apples thoroughly under cold water and pat them dry with a clean kitchen towel.
2. Core the apples and slice them into thin wedges or rounds, removing any seeds.
3. If you're not serving the apple slices immediately, you can squeeze a little lemon juice over them to prevent browning.
4. Place the almond butter in a small microwave-safe bowl. If the almond butter is too thick, you can microwave it for 15-20 seconds to soften it slightly.
5. If desired, stir in honey or maple syrup and cinnamon into the almond butter for added sweetness and flavor.
6. Arrange the apple slices on a serving plate or platter.
7. Using a spoon or knife, spread a generous amount of almond butter onto each apple slice.
8. Serve immediately and enjoy these delicious apple slices with almond butter as a nutritious snack for school or work!

**Veggie Sticks with Hummus**

Ingredients:

- 2 large carrots
- 2 large celery stalks
- 1 red bell pepper
- 1 yellow bell pepper
- 1 cucumber
- 1 cup hummus (store-bought or homemade)
- Fresh parsley or cilantro for garnish (optional)

Instructions:

1. Wash all the vegetables thoroughly under cold water and pat them dry with a clean kitchen towel.
2. Peel the carrots and trim off the ends. Cut them into long, thin sticks.
3. Trim off the ends of the celery stalks and cut them into sticks of similar length to the carrots.
4. Core the bell peppers, remove the seeds, and slice them into strips.
5. Peel the cucumber (if desired) and cut it into thin rounds or sticks.
6. Arrange the prepared vegetable sticks on a serving platter or plate.
7. Place the hummus in a bowl and place it in the center of the platter.
8. If desired, garnish the hummus with fresh parsley or cilantro for a pop of color.
9. Serve the veggie sticks with hummus as a healthy and satisfying snack for school or work. Enjoy dipping the crunchy vegetables into the creamy hummus!

**Greek Yogurt Parfait with Berries and Granola**

Ingredients:

- 1 cup Greek yogurt (plain or flavored)
- 1/2 cup mixed berries (such as strawberries, blueberries, raspberries)
- 1/4 cup granola (store-bought or homemade)
- Honey or maple syrup (optional, for drizzling)
- Fresh mint leaves for garnish (optional)

Instructions:

1. In a serving glass or bowl, start by adding a layer of Greek yogurt at the bottom.
2. Wash the mixed berries under cold water and pat them dry with a clean kitchen towel. If using strawberries, remove the stems and slice them.
3. Add a layer of mixed berries on top of the Greek yogurt.
4. Sprinkle a layer of granola over the berries.
5. Repeat the layers - add another layer of Greek yogurt, followed by mixed berries, and finish with a final layer of granola on top.
6. If desired, drizzle honey or maple syrup over the top for added sweetness.
7. Garnish with fresh mint leaves for a burst of freshness and color.
8. Serve the Greek yogurt parfait immediately as a nutritious and delicious snack for school or work. Enjoy the creamy yogurt, sweet berries, and crunchy granola in every spoonful!

**Roasted Chickpeas with Seasonings**

Ingredients:

- 2 cans (15 ounces each) chickpeas (garbanzo beans), drained and rinsed
- 2 tablespoons olive oil
- 1 teaspoon ground cumin
- 1 teaspoon smoked paprika
- 1/2 teaspoon garlic powder
- 1/2 teaspoon onion powder
- 1/2 teaspoon chili powder (optional, for added heat)
- Salt and black pepper, to taste

Instructions:

1. Preheat your oven to 400°F (200°C). Line a large baking sheet with parchment paper or aluminum foil.
2. Drain and rinse the chickpeas thoroughly under cold water. Pat them dry with a clean kitchen towel or paper towels to remove excess moisture.
3. In a large mixing bowl, toss the chickpeas with olive oil until they are evenly coated.
4. In a small bowl, combine the ground cumin, smoked paprika, garlic powder, onion powder, and chili powder (if using). Stir to mix well.
5. Sprinkle the seasoning mixture over the chickpeas and toss until they are evenly coated with the spices.
6. Spread the seasoned chickpeas in a single layer on the prepared baking sheet.
7. Roast the chickpeas in the preheated oven for 20-25 minutes, stirring halfway through, or until they are golden brown and crispy.
8. Once roasted, remove the baking sheet from the oven and let the chickpeas cool slightly before serving.
9. Season the roasted chickpeas with salt and black pepper to taste.
10. Serve the roasted chickpeas with seasonings as a crunchy and flavorful snack for school or work. Enjoy their deliciously spiced flavor and satisfying crunch!

**Banana Oatmeal Muffins**

Ingredients:

- 1 cup mashed ripe bananas (about 2-3 bananas)
- 1/4 cup maple syrup or honey
- 1/4 cup unsweetened applesauce
- 1/4 cup almond milk or any milk of your choice
- 1 teaspoon vanilla extract
- 1 1/2 cups rolled oats
- 1/2 cup whole wheat flour or all-purpose flour
- 1 teaspoon baking powder
- 1/2 teaspoon baking soda
- 1/2 teaspoon ground cinnamon
- 1/4 teaspoon salt
- Optional add-ins: chopped nuts, chocolate chips, dried fruit, etc.

Instructions:

1. Preheat your oven to 350°F (175°C). Line a muffin tin with paper liners or grease the muffin cups lightly with oil.
2. In a large mixing bowl, combine the mashed bananas, maple syrup (or honey), applesauce, almond milk, and vanilla extract. Mix until well combined.
3. In another bowl, whisk together the rolled oats, flour, baking powder, baking soda, ground cinnamon, and salt.
4. Gradually add the dry ingredients to the wet ingredients, stirring until just combined. Be careful not to overmix.
5. If desired, fold in any optional add-ins such as chopped nuts, chocolate chips, or dried fruit.
6. Divide the batter evenly among the prepared muffin cups, filling each cup about 3/4 full.
7. Bake the muffins in the preheated oven for 18-22 minutes, or until a toothpick inserted into the center comes out clean.
8. Once baked, remove the muffins from the oven and allow them to cool in the muffin tin for a few minutes before transferring them to a wire rack to cool completely.

These Banana Oatmeal Muffins are moist, flavorful, and packed with wholesome ingredients. They're perfect for a grab-and-go breakfast or a healthy snack any time of the day. Enjoy!

**Rice Cakes with Avocado and Tomato Slices**

Ingredients:

- Rice cakes
- 1 ripe avocado
- 1-2 tomatoes, sliced
- Salt and pepper to taste
- Optional toppings: red pepper flakes, sesame seeds, balsamic glaze, lime juice, etc.

Instructions:

1. Begin by slicing the avocado in half and removing the pit. Scoop out the flesh into a bowl and mash it with a fork until smooth.
2. Season the mashed avocado with salt and pepper to taste, and any additional optional toppings you desire, such as lime juice or red pepper flakes.
3. Spread a generous amount of the mashed avocado mixture onto each rice cake.
4. Top the avocado spread with slices of fresh tomato. You can arrange the tomato slices in a single layer or overlap them slightly, depending on your preference.
5. Optionally, sprinkle some additional salt and pepper over the tomato slices, or add more toppings like sesame seeds or a drizzle of balsamic glaze for extra flavor.
6. Serve the rice cakes with avocado and tomato slices immediately as a snack or light meal.

These rice cakes with avocado and tomato slices are simple, delicious, and packed with nutritious ingredients. They're perfect for a quick and easy snack or a light lunch on the go. Feel free to customize the toppings to suit your taste preferences!

## Popcorn (lightly salted or flavored with nutritional yeast)

Lightly Salted Popcorn:

Ingredients:

- 1/4 cup popcorn kernels
- 1-2 tablespoons vegetable oil (such as canola or coconut oil)
- Salt to taste

Instructions:

1. Heat the vegetable oil in a large pot over medium heat. Add a few popcorn kernels to the pot and cover it with a lid.
2. Once the test kernels have popped, add the remaining popcorn kernels to the pot in an even layer. Cover the pot with the lid.
3. Shake the pot occasionally to prevent the popcorn from burning. Continue cooking until the popping slows down to about 2-3 seconds between pops.
4. Remove the pot from the heat and carefully remove the lid, allowing any remaining steam to escape.
5. Transfer the popcorn to a large bowl and season it with salt to taste. Toss the popcorn gently to distribute the salt evenly.
6. Serve the lightly salted popcorn immediately and enjoy!

Popcorn Flavored with Nutritional Yeast:

Ingredients:

- 1/4 cup popcorn kernels
- 1-2 tablespoons vegetable oil
- Nutritional yeast
- Salt to taste

Instructions:

1. Heat the vegetable oil in a large pot over medium heat. Add a few popcorn kernels to the pot and cover it with a lid.
2. Once the test kernels have popped, add the remaining popcorn kernels to the pot in an even layer. Cover the pot with the lid.
3. Shake the pot occasionally to prevent the popcorn from burning. Continue cooking until the popping slows down to about 2-3 seconds between pops.

4. Remove the pot from the heat and carefully remove the lid, allowing any remaining steam to escape.
5. Transfer the popcorn to a large bowl. Drizzle it with a little more vegetable oil and toss gently to coat.
6. Sprinkle nutritional yeast over the popcorn, tossing gently to coat evenly. Add salt to taste.
7. Serve the popcorn flavored with nutritional yeast immediately for a savory and satisfying snack.

These popcorn recipes are simple yet delicious, providing options for both a classic lightly salted version and a flavorful variation with nutritional yeast. Enjoy your snack!

**Edamame (steamed and lightly salted)**

Ingredients:

- Edamame pods (fresh or frozen)
- Salt (to taste)

Instructions:

1. If using frozen edamame, thaw them by placing them in a bowl of cold water for a few minutes.
2. Rinse the edamame pods under cold water to remove any dirt or debris.
3. Bring a pot of water to a boil. Add a generous amount of salt to the boiling water.
4. Once the water is boiling, add the edamame pods to the pot. Cook for about 3-5 minutes, or until the pods are tender.
5. Drain the edamame pods and transfer them to a serving bowl.
6. Sprinkle the steamed edamame with a little more salt, tossing gently to coat evenly.
7. Serve the steamed and lightly salted edamame immediately as a snack or appetizer.

Steamed edamame is not only delicious but also packed with protein, fiber, and essential nutrients. Enjoy this healthy snack any time of the day!

**Cottage Cheese with Pineapple Chunks**

Ingredients:

- Cottage cheese
- Fresh pineapple chunks (or canned pineapple chunks, drained)
- Optional: honey or maple syrup (for drizzling)

Instructions:

1. Scoop the desired amount of cottage cheese into a serving bowl.
2. Add fresh pineapple chunks on top of the cottage cheese.
3. If using canned pineapple chunks, make sure to drain them well before adding them to the cottage cheese.
4. Optional: Drizzle a little honey or maple syrup over the cottage cheese and pineapple for added sweetness.
5. Gently toss the cottage cheese and pineapple together to combine.
6. Serve immediately and enjoy as a refreshing snack or light meal.

This cottage cheese with pineapple chunks is a simple yet delicious combination that offers a mix of creamy, tangy, and sweet flavors. It's perfect for a quick breakfast, snack, or even as a light dessert option. Feel free to adjust the sweetness according to your taste preferences.

**Whole Grain Crackers with Sliced Cheese**

Ingredients:

- Whole grain crackers (such as whole wheat or multigrain)
- Sliced cheese (such as cheddar, Swiss, or gouda)
- Optional: Thinly sliced apple or pear, grapes, nuts, honey, or mustard for serving

Instructions:

1. Arrange the whole grain crackers on a serving platter or plate.
2. Place a slice of cheese on each cracker. You can use a single type of cheese or mix and match different varieties for variety.
3. If desired, add optional toppings such as thinly sliced apple or pear, grapes, nuts, honey, or mustard on top of the cheese.
4. Serve the whole grain crackers with sliced cheese immediately as a snack or appetizer.

This combination of whole grain crackers with sliced cheese is versatile and customizable, making it perfect for entertaining or a quick and easy snack any time of the day. Feel free to experiment with different types of crackers, cheeses, and toppings to suit your taste preferences!

**Fruit Kabobs (skewered mixed fruit)**

Ingredients:

- Assorted fruits, such as:
    - Strawberries, hulled
    - Pineapple chunks
    - Grapes
    - Watermelon cubes
    - Cantaloupe or honeydew melon cubes
    - Kiwi slices
    - Blueberries
    - Banana slices (dipped in lemon juice to prevent browning, if desired)
- Wooden skewers

Instructions:

1. Prepare the fruits by washing them thoroughly and cutting them into bite-sized pieces or slices.
2. Thread the fruit onto wooden skewers in any order you like, alternating between different types of fruit to create colorful patterns.
3. Leave a little space at the ends of the skewers for easy handling.
4. Repeat the process until you've used up all your fruit and filled the skewers.
5. Arrange the fruit kabobs on a serving platter or plate.
6. Optional: You can serve the fruit kabobs with a dipping sauce, such as yogurt, honey, or melted chocolate, on the side for added flavor.
7. Serve the fruit kabobs immediately as a refreshing snack or dessert option.

These fruit kabobs are not only delicious but also visually appealing, making them perfect for parties, picnics, or simply as a healthy treat to enjoy at home. Feel free to customize the fruit selection according to your preferences and what's in season.

**Almond Energy Balls**

Ingredients:

- 1 cup almonds
- 1 cup pitted dates
- 1/4 cup almond butter
- 2 tablespoons unsweetened cocoa powder
- 1 teaspoon vanilla extract
- Pinch of salt
- Optional: shredded coconut, chia seeds, or chopped nuts for coating

Instructions:

1. In a food processor, pulse the almonds until finely ground into a coarse meal.
2. Add the pitted dates, almond butter, cocoa powder, vanilla extract, and a pinch of salt to the food processor.
3. Process the mixture until it forms a sticky dough-like consistency. If the mixture seems too dry, you can add a splash of water to help it come together.
4. Once the mixture is well combined and forms a dough, use your hands to roll it into small balls, about 1 inch in diameter.
5. Optional: Roll the energy balls in shredded coconut, chia seeds, or chopped nuts for added texture and flavor.
6. Place the almond energy balls on a baking sheet lined with parchment paper, and refrigerate them for at least 30 minutes to firm up.
7. Once chilled, transfer the energy balls to an airtight container and store them in the refrigerator for up to one week.

These almond energy balls are packed with protein, fiber, and healthy fats, making them a great snack option for when you need a quick energy boost. Enjoy them as a pre-workout snack, a midday pick-me-up, or a healthy dessert alternative!

**Quinoa Salad Cups**

Ingredients:

- 1 cup quinoa, rinsed
- 2 cups water or vegetable broth
- 1 cup cherry tomatoes, halved
- 1 cucumber, diced
- 1 bell pepper, diced
- 1/4 cup red onion, finely chopped
- 1/4 cup fresh parsley, chopped
- 1/4 cup fresh mint leaves, chopped
- Juice of 1 lemon
- 2 tablespoons extra virgin olive oil
- Salt and pepper to taste
- Optional: crumbled feta cheese, chopped avocado, olives, or any other desired toppings

Instructions:

1. In a medium saucepan, combine the quinoa and water or vegetable broth. Bring to a boil, then reduce the heat to low, cover, and simmer for about 15-20 minutes, or until the quinoa is cooked and the liquid is absorbed. Remove from heat and let it cool slightly.
2. In a large mixing bowl, combine the cooked quinoa, cherry tomatoes, cucumber, bell pepper, red onion, parsley, and mint.
3. In a small bowl, whisk together the lemon juice, extra virgin olive oil, salt, and pepper to make the dressing.
4. Pour the dressing over the quinoa salad mixture and toss gently to coat everything evenly.
5. Taste and adjust seasoning if needed.
6. To assemble the quinoa salad cups, spoon the quinoa salad mixture into individual lettuce cups or small bowls.
7. If desired, top each quinoa salad cup with crumbled feta cheese, chopped avocado, olives, or any other desired toppings.
8. Serve immediately as a light meal or snack, or refrigerate until ready to serve.

These quinoa salad cups are versatile and customizable, so feel free to adjust the ingredients and toppings according to your preferences. They're perfect for a healthy lunch, appetizer, or party snack!

**Baked Sweet Potato Fries**

Ingredients:

- 2 large sweet potatoes
- 2 tablespoons olive oil
- 1 teaspoon paprika
- 1/2 teaspoon garlic powder
- 1/2 teaspoon onion powder
- 1/2 teaspoon salt
- 1/4 teaspoon black pepper
- Optional: chopped fresh parsley or grated Parmesan cheese for garnish

Instructions:

1. Preheat your oven to 425°F (220°C) and line a baking sheet with parchment paper or aluminum foil.
2. Wash and peel the sweet potatoes. Cut them into thin strips, about 1/4 inch thick.
3. In a large bowl, toss the sweet potato strips with olive oil, paprika, garlic powder, onion powder, salt, and black pepper until evenly coated.
4. Spread the seasoned sweet potato strips in a single layer on the prepared baking sheet, making sure they're not overlapping.
5. Bake in the preheated oven for 20-25 minutes, flipping the fries halfway through, until they're golden brown and crispy.
6. Once baked, remove the sweet potato fries from the oven and let them cool slightly.
7. Optional: Sprinkle the baked sweet potato fries with chopped fresh parsley or grated Parmesan cheese for extra flavor.
8. Serve the baked sweet potato fries hot as a side dish or snack, with your favorite dipping sauce such as ketchup, aioli, or sriracha mayo.

These baked sweet potato fries are crispy on the outside, tender on the inside, and packed with flavor. They're a healthier alternative to fried potatoes and make a delicious addition to any meal!

**Cucumber Slices with Tzatziki Sauce**

Ingredients:

- 1 large cucumber
- Tzatziki sauce (store-bought or homemade, see below)
- Optional garnish: chopped fresh dill, parsley, or mint leaves

For the Tzatziki Sauce:

- 1 cup Greek yogurt
- 1/2 cucumber, grated and squeezed to remove excess moisture
- 2 cloves garlic, minced
- 1 tablespoon extra virgin olive oil
- 1 tablespoon fresh lemon juice
- 1 tablespoon chopped fresh dill (or mint)
- Salt and pepper to taste

Instructions:

For the Tzatziki Sauce:

1. In a mixing bowl, combine the Greek yogurt, grated cucumber, minced garlic, olive oil, lemon juice, and chopped fresh dill.
2. Season with salt and pepper to taste. Stir until all the ingredients are well combined.
3. Cover the bowl with plastic wrap and refrigerate for at least 1 hour to allow the flavors to meld together.

For the Cucumber Slices with Tzatziki Sauce:

1. Wash the cucumber and slice it into thin rounds.
2. Arrange the cucumber slices on a serving platter or plate.
3. Spoon the tzatziki sauce into a small bowl and place it in the center of the platter, or you can dollop the sauce onto each cucumber slice individually.
4. Optional: Garnish the tzatziki sauce with chopped fresh dill, parsley, or mint leaves for extra flavor and presentation.
5. Serve the cucumber slices with tzatziki sauce immediately as a refreshing snack or appetizer.

These cucumber slices with tzatziki sauce are light, crunchy, and bursting with fresh flavors. They're perfect for serving at parties, gatherings, or as a healthy snack any time of the day. Enjoy!

**Chia Seed Pudding with Mixed Berries**

Ingredients:

- 1/4 cup chia seeds
- 1 cup unsweetened almond milk (or any milk of your choice)
- 1 tablespoon maple syrup or honey (optional, adjust to taste)
- 1/2 teaspoon vanilla extract
- Mixed berries (such as strawberries, blueberries, raspberries, blackberries)
- Optional toppings: sliced almonds, shredded coconut, or granola

Instructions:

1. In a mixing bowl, combine the chia seeds, almond milk, maple syrup or honey (if using), and vanilla extract. Stir well to combine all the ingredients.
2. Let the mixture sit for a few minutes, then stir again to prevent clumping. Cover the bowl and refrigerate for at least 2 hours, or overnight, to allow the chia seeds to absorb the liquid and thicken.
3. Once the chia pudding has thickened to your desired consistency, give it a good stir to break up any clumps.
4. Wash and prepare the mixed berries. You can slice the strawberries and leave the other berries whole.
5. To serve, divide the chia seed pudding into individual serving bowls or jars.
6. Top each serving of chia seed pudding with a generous portion of mixed berries.
7. Optional: Sprinkle sliced almonds, shredded coconut, or granola over the mixed berries for added texture and flavor.
8. Serve the chia seed pudding with mixed berries immediately as a delicious and nutritious dessert or breakfast option.

This chia seed pudding with mixed berries is packed with fiber, protein, and antioxidants, making it a healthy and satisfying treat. It's also customizable, so feel free to adjust the sweetness and toppings according to your preferences. Enjoy!

**Mixed Nuts (unsalted)**

Ingredients:

- Assorted nuts of your choice, such as:
    - Almonds
    - Walnuts
    - Cashews
    - Pecans
    - Brazil nuts
    - Hazelnuts
    - Macadamia nuts
- Optional: pistachios, pine nuts, or any other nuts you like

Instructions:

1. Preheat your oven to 300°F (150°C).
2. Spread the assorted nuts in a single layer on a baking sheet lined with parchment paper or a silicone baking mat.
3. Bake the nuts in the preheated oven for about 10-15 minutes, stirring occasionally, until they are lightly toasted and fragrant. Keep an eye on them to prevent burning.
4. Once the nuts are toasted to your liking, remove them from the oven and let them cool completely.
5. Once cooled, transfer the unsalted mixed nuts to an airtight container for storage.
6. Enjoy the mixed nuts as a healthy snack, or use them in salads, trail mix, granola, or other recipes.

These unsalted mixed nuts are a great source of healthy fats, protein, vitamins, and minerals. They're perfect for munching on between meals or as a topping for various dishes. Feel free to customize the mix by including your favorite nuts!

**Whole Grain Toast with Mashed Avocado**

Ingredients:

- Whole grain bread slices
- Ripe avocados
- Lemon juice (optional)
- Salt and black pepper to taste
- Optional toppings: red pepper flakes, cherry tomatoes, sliced radishes, microgreens, poached egg, or crumbled feta cheese

Instructions:

1. Toast the whole grain bread slices until golden brown and crispy.
2. While the bread is toasting, prepare the mashed avocado. Cut the ripe avocados in half, remove the pits, and scoop the flesh into a bowl.
3. Mash the avocado with a fork until smooth or slightly chunky, depending on your preference.
4. If desired, add a squeeze of lemon juice to the mashed avocado to prevent browning and add a fresh flavor. Season with salt and black pepper to taste.
5. Once the toast is done, spread a generous amount of mashed avocado onto each slice.
6. Optional: Top the avocado toast with your choice of toppings, such as red pepper flakes, cherry tomatoes, sliced radishes, microgreens, poached egg, or crumbled feta cheese.
7. Serve the whole grain toast with mashed avocado immediately as a delicious and nutritious breakfast or snack.

This whole grain toast with mashed avocado is rich in healthy fats, fiber, and vitamins, making it a satisfying and wholesome option to start your day. Feel free to get creative with the toppings to suit your taste preferences!

**Greek Yogurt Dip with Pretzel Sticks**

Ingredients:

- 1 cup Greek yogurt
- 1 tablespoon lemon juice
- 1 clove garlic, minced
- 1 tablespoon chopped fresh dill (or 1 teaspoon dried dill)
- 1 tablespoon chopped fresh parsley
- Salt and pepper to taste
- Pretzel sticks for dipping

Instructions:

1. In a mixing bowl, combine the Greek yogurt, lemon juice, minced garlic, chopped fresh dill, and chopped fresh parsley.
2. Stir the ingredients together until well combined.
3. Season the Greek yogurt dip with salt and pepper to taste. Adjust the seasoning according to your preferences.
4. Transfer the dip to a serving bowl and garnish with a sprig of fresh dill or parsley, if desired.
5. Serve the Greek yogurt dip with pretzel sticks for dipping.

This Greek yogurt dip is creamy, tangy, and packed with flavor, making it the perfect accompaniment to salty pretzel sticks. It's also a healthier alternative to store-bought dips, as Greek yogurt is rich in protein and probiotics. Enjoy this delicious snack at parties, gatherings, or as a tasty treat for yourself!

**Carrot Cake Energy Bites**

Ingredients:

- 1 cup rolled oats
- 1/2 cup shredded carrots
- 1/4 cup chopped walnuts or pecans
- 1/4 cup shredded coconut
- 1/4 cup raisins or chopped dates
- 2 tablespoons maple syrup or honey
- 2 tablespoons almond butter or any nut butter of your choice
- 1 teaspoon vanilla extract
- 1/2 teaspoon ground cinnamon
- 1/4 teaspoon ground nutmeg
- Pinch of salt

Instructions:

1. In a food processor, pulse the rolled oats until they are finely ground into a coarse flour-like consistency.
2. Add the shredded carrots, chopped nuts, shredded coconut, raisins or chopped dates, maple syrup or honey, almond butter, vanilla extract, ground cinnamon, ground nutmeg, and a pinch of salt to the food processor.
3. Process the mixture until it comes together and forms a sticky dough-like consistency.
4. If the mixture seems too dry, you can add a splash of water to help it come together.
5. Once the mixture is well combined, scoop out tablespoon-sized portions and roll them into balls using your hands.
6. Place the carrot cake energy bites on a baking sheet lined with parchment paper.
7. Optional: Roll the energy bites in additional shredded coconut or chopped nuts for coating, if desired.
8. Refrigerate the carrot cake energy bites for at least 30 minutes to firm up before serving.
9. Once chilled, transfer the energy bites to an airtight container and store them in the refrigerator for up to one week.

These carrot cake energy bites are packed with wholesome ingredients like oats, carrots, nuts, and dried fruit, making them a healthy and satisfying snack option. They're perfect for a quick energy boost on the go or as a sweet treat any time of the day!

**Seaweed Snacks**

Ingredients:

- Roasted seaweed sheets (nori)
- Optional: sesame oil, soy sauce, or other seasonings of your choice

Instructions:

1. If your seaweed sheets are not already seasoned, you can customize them by brushing lightly with sesame oil or spraying with soy sauce. Be cautious not to oversaturate them, as they can become too salty.
2. Cut the seaweed sheets into smaller pieces if desired, such as strips or squares, using kitchen scissors.
3. Serve the seaweed snacks immediately, or store them in an airtight container for later consumption.

These seaweed snacks are low in calories and packed with nutrients, including vitamins, minerals, and antioxidants. They make a delicious and satisfying snack on their own, or you can pair them with other items like rice, sushi, or salads for added flavor and texture. Enjoy the unique taste of seaweed in a convenient and portable snack form!

**Whole Grain Pita Chips with Hummus**

Ingredients:

- Whole grain pita bread
- Olive oil
- Salt
- Hummus (store-bought or homemade)

Instructions:

1. Preheat your oven to 375°F (190°C).
2. Cut the whole grain pita bread into wedges or triangles using a knife or kitchen scissors.
3. Place the pita wedges on a baking sheet lined with parchment paper.
4. Lightly brush both sides of the pita wedges with olive oil and sprinkle with salt.
5. Bake the pita chips in the preheated oven for about 8-10 minutes, or until they are golden brown and crispy. Keep an eye on them to prevent burning.
6. Once the pita chips are done, remove them from the oven and let them cool slightly.
7. Serve the whole grain pita chips with hummus for dipping.

These whole grain pita chips are crunchy and flavorful, and they pair perfectly with creamy hummus. They're also a healthier alternative to regular chips, as they're made with whole grain pita bread and baked instead of fried. Enjoy this delicious snack any time of the day!

**Frozen Grapes**

Ingredients:

- Grapes (any variety)

Instructions:

1. Start by washing the grapes thoroughly under cold water to remove any dirt or residue.
2. Pat the grapes dry with a paper towel or clean kitchen towel.
3. Spread the grapes out on a baking sheet lined with parchment paper or wax paper. Make sure they're in a single layer and not touching each other.
4. Place the baking sheet in the freezer and freeze the grapes for at least 2-3 hours, or until they're completely frozen.
5. Once the grapes are frozen solid, transfer them to a resealable plastic bag or an airtight container for storage in the freezer.
6. Serve the frozen grapes straight from the freezer as a refreshing snack.

These frozen grapes have a satisfyingly icy texture and a burst of natural sweetness. They're a healthier alternative to sugary popsicles or ice cream and make a delightful treat for both kids and adults. Enjoy them on their own or as a topping for yogurt, smoothie bowls, or desserts!

**Mini Caprese Skewers (cherry tomatoes, mozzarella, basil)**

Ingredients:

- Cherry tomatoes
- Fresh mini mozzarella balls (bocconcini or ciliegine)
- Fresh basil leaves
- Balsamic glaze (optional)
- Wooden skewers

Instructions:

1. Rinse the cherry tomatoes and basil leaves under cold water, and pat them dry with a paper towel.
2. Drain any excess liquid from the mozzarella balls.
3. Assemble the skewers by threading one cherry tomato, one mini mozzarella ball, and one basil leaf onto each skewer, repeating the pattern until all ingredients are used.
4. Arrange the assembled Caprese skewers on a serving platter or plate.
5. Optional: Drizzle balsamic glaze over the skewers for added flavor and presentation.
6. Serve the mini Caprese skewers immediately as a tasty appetizer or snack.

These mini Caprese skewers are not only visually appealing but also bursting with fresh flavors. They're perfect for parties, gatherings, or as a light and refreshing snack any time of the day. Enjoy the combination of juicy tomatoes, creamy mozzarella, and aromatic basil in each bite!

**Kale Chips**

Ingredients:

- 1 bunch of kale
- Olive oil
- Salt (optional)
- Optional seasonings: garlic powder, onion powder, paprika, nutritional yeast, or grated Parmesan cheese

Instructions:

1. Preheat your oven to 275°F (135°C).
2. Wash the kale leaves thoroughly under cold water and pat them dry with a clean kitchen towel or paper towels. Make sure the leaves are completely dry to ensure crispiness.
3. Remove the tough stems from the kale leaves and tear the leaves into bite-sized pieces.
4. Place the torn kale leaves in a large mixing bowl.
5. Drizzle a small amount of olive oil over the kale leaves, using your hands to massage the oil evenly onto the leaves. Be careful not to use too much oil, as it can make the chips greasy.
6. Sprinkle salt and any desired seasonings over the kale leaves, tossing gently to coat them evenly.
7. Arrange the seasoned kale leaves in a single layer on a baking sheet lined with parchment paper or a silicone baking mat. Make sure the leaves are not overlapping to ensure even baking.
8. Bake the kale chips in the preheated oven for about 20-25 minutes, or until they are crisp and slightly golden brown around the edges. Keep an eye on them during the last few minutes of baking to prevent burning.
9. Once the kale chips are done, remove them from the oven and let them cool on the baking sheet for a few minutes.
10. Transfer the kale chips to a serving bowl or container and serve them immediately as a healthy and flavorful snack.

These homemade kale chips are crunchy, savory, and packed with nutrients. They're perfect for munching on between meals or as a guilt-free snack option. Feel free to customize the seasonings to suit your taste preferences!

**Whole Grain Banana Bread**

Ingredients:

- 2 ripe bananas, mashed
- 1/3 cup melted coconut oil or vegetable oil
- 1/2 cup maple syrup or honey
- 2 eggs
- 1/4 cup milk (dairy or non-dairy)
- 1 teaspoon vanilla extract
- 1 3/4 cups whole wheat flour or whole grain flour of your choice
- 1 teaspoon baking soda
- 1/2 teaspoon salt
- Optional add-ins: chopped nuts, chocolate chips, or dried fruit

Instructions:

1. Preheat your oven to 350°F (175°C). Grease a 9x5-inch loaf pan or line it with parchment paper.
2. In a large mixing bowl, combine the mashed bananas, melted coconut oil or vegetable oil, maple syrup or honey, eggs, milk, and vanilla extract. Mix until well combined.
3. In a separate bowl, whisk together the whole wheat flour, baking soda, and salt.
4. Add the dry ingredients to the wet ingredients and stir until just combined. Be careful not to overmix.
5. If desired, fold in any optional add-ins such as chopped nuts, chocolate chips, or dried fruit.
6. Pour the batter into the prepared loaf pan and spread it out evenly.
7. Bake in the preheated oven for 50-60 minutes, or until a toothpick inserted into the center of the bread comes out clean.
8. Once done, remove the banana bread from the oven and let it cool in the pan for 10 minutes. Then, transfer it to a wire rack to cool completely before slicing.

This whole grain banana bread is moist, flavorful, and packed with fiber and nutrients from the whole wheat flour and bananas. It's a healthier twist on the classic banana bread recipe, perfect for enjoying any time of day!

**Bell Pepper Slices with Guacamole**

Ingredients:

- Bell peppers (assorted colors)
- Ripe avocados
- Lime juice
- Salt and pepper to taste
- Optional toppings: chopped tomatoes, diced onions, minced garlic, cilantro, jalapeño slices, or crumbled feta cheese

Instructions:

1. Start by washing the bell peppers under cold water, then pat them dry with a paper towel. Slice the bell peppers into strips or wedges, removing the seeds and membranes.
2. Cut the avocados in half, remove the pits, and scoop the flesh into a bowl.
3. Mash the avocados with a fork until smooth or slightly chunky, depending on your preference.
4. Add lime juice, salt, and pepper to taste to the mashed avocado and stir until well combined.
5. Optional: Add any additional toppings or seasonings to the guacamole, such as chopped tomatoes, diced onions, minced garlic, cilantro, jalapeño slices, or crumbled feta cheese.
6. Arrange the bell pepper slices on a serving platter or plate.
7. Serve the bell pepper slices with the guacamole for dipping.

These bell pepper slices with guacamole are a colorful and flavorful snack that's packed with vitamins, minerals, and healthy fats. They're perfect for parties, gatherings, or as a tasty and nutritious treat any time of the day. Enjoy the combination of crunchy bell peppers and creamy guacamole!

**Homemade Fruit Leather**

Ingredients:

- 4 cups of fresh fruit (such as strawberries, peaches, apples, or berries)
- 1-2 tablespoons of honey or maple syrup (optional, depending on the sweetness of the fruit)
- Lemon juice (optional, to prevent browning)

Instructions:

1. Preheat your oven to the lowest temperature setting (usually around 140°F or 60°C). If your oven doesn't go that low, you can prop the door open slightly to allow air circulation.
2. Wash and chop the fruit into small pieces, removing any pits, seeds, or stems.
3. Puree the fruit in a blender or food processor until smooth. If the fruit is very thick, you can add a little water to help it blend.
4. Taste the puree and adjust the sweetness if necessary by adding honey or maple syrup. You can also add a splash of lemon juice to enhance the flavor and prevent browning.
5. Line a baking sheet with parchment paper or a silicone baking mat, making sure it's flat and smooth.
6. Pour the fruit puree onto the prepared baking sheet, spreading it out evenly with a spatula until it's about 1/8 to 1/4 inch thick.
7. Place the baking sheet in the preheated oven and bake the fruit puree for 4-6 hours, or until it's no longer sticky to the touch and can be peeled away from the parchment paper easily.
8. Once the fruit leather is done, remove it from the oven and let it cool completely on the baking sheet.
9. Once cooled, use kitchen scissors or a knife to cut the fruit leather into strips or squares.
10. Roll up the fruit leather strips with parchment paper or plastic wrap and store them in an airtight container at room temperature for up to a week, or in the refrigerator for longer storage.

Homemade fruit leather is a fun and healthy snack that's perfect for kids and adults alike. You can experiment with different fruit combinations and flavors to suit your taste preferences. Enjoy this homemade treat as a delicious and nutritious snack any time of the day!

**Almond Butter Rice Cake Sandwiches**

Ingredients:

- Rice cakes
- Almond butter (or any nut butter of your choice)
- Optional toppings: sliced banana, berries, honey, cinnamon, chia seeds, or shredded coconut

Instructions:

1. Spread a layer of almond butter (or your chosen nut butter) onto one rice cake.
2. If desired, add additional toppings such as sliced banana, berries, honey, cinnamon, chia seeds, or shredded coconut on top of the almond butter.
3. Place another rice cake on top to form a sandwich.
4. Repeat the process to make additional almond butter rice cake sandwiches.
5. Serve immediately, or wrap each sandwich individually in plastic wrap or foil for later enjoyment.

These almond butter rice cake sandwiches are a quick and easy snack that's packed with protein, fiber, and healthy fats. They're perfect for a mid-morning or afternoon pick-me-up, or as a pre- or post-workout snack. Feel free to get creative with the toppings to suit your taste preferences!

**Berry Smoothie Popsicles**

Ingredients:

- 1 cup mixed berries (such as strawberries, blueberries, raspberries, and blackberries)
- 1 ripe banana
- 1 cup plain Greek yogurt
- 1-2 tablespoons honey or maple syrup (optional, depending on sweetness preference)
- 1/2 cup milk (dairy or non-dairy)
- Popsicle molds
- Popsicle sticks

Instructions:

1. Wash the mixed berries and remove any stems or hulls.
2. Peel the ripe banana and slice it into chunks.
3. In a blender, combine the mixed berries, banana chunks, Greek yogurt, honey or maple syrup (if using), and milk.
4. Blend the ingredients until smooth and well combined. If the mixture is too thick, you can add more milk to reach your desired consistency.
5. Taste the berry smoothie mixture and adjust the sweetness if necessary by adding more honey or maple syrup.
6. Once the smoothie mixture is ready, pour it into the popsicle molds, filling them almost to the top.
7. Insert popsicle sticks into the molds.
8. Place the popsicle molds in the freezer and freeze the berry smoothie popsicles for at least 4-6 hours, or until they are completely frozen.
9. Once frozen, remove the popsicle molds from the freezer and run them under warm water for a few seconds to help release the popsicles.
10. Carefully remove the berry smoothie popsicles from the molds and enjoy them immediately, or store them in a resealable plastic bag or container in the freezer for later enjoyment.

These berry smoothie popsicles are a healthy and refreshing treat that's packed with vitamins, minerals, and antioxidants from the mixed berries. They're perfect for kids and adults alike, and you can customize the recipe by using your favorite berries and adjusting the sweetness to suit your taste preferences. Enjoy these delicious popsicles as a cool and satisfying snack or dessert on hot summer days!

**Celery Sticks with Peanut Butter and Raisins**

Ingredients:

- Celery stalks
- Peanut butter (or any nut or seed butter of your choice)
- Raisins (or any dried fruit of your choice)

Instructions:

1. Wash the celery stalks thoroughly under cold water and pat them dry with a paper towel.
2. Cut the celery stalks into manageable lengths, typically about 3-4 inches long.
3. Spread peanut butter (or your chosen nut or seed butter) onto each celery stick, filling the center groove where the celery ribbons are.
4. Place raisins (or your chosen dried fruit) onto the peanut butter, pressing them lightly so they stick.
5. Repeat the process for each celery stick until you have as many "Ants on a Log" as desired.
6. Serve the celery sticks with peanut butter and raisins immediately as a delicious and nutritious snack.

These celery sticks with peanut butter and raisins are not only fun to eat but also packed with protein, fiber, and vitamins. They make for a satisfying and energizing snack that's perfect for curbing hunger cravings between meals or as a tasty addition to lunchboxes. Enjoy this classic snack combination any time of the day!

**Spinach and Feta Mini Frittatas**

Ingredients:

- 6 large eggs
- 1/4 cup milk (dairy or non-dairy)
- 1 cup fresh spinach, chopped
- 1/4 cup crumbled feta cheese
- 1/4 cup diced red bell pepper
- 2 tablespoons diced onion
- 1 tablespoon chopped fresh herbs (such as parsley, chives, or basil)
- Salt and pepper to taste
- Cooking spray or olive oil for greasing the muffin tin

Instructions:

1. Preheat your oven to 375°F (190°C). Grease a 12-cup muffin tin with cooking spray or olive oil.
2. In a large mixing bowl, whisk together the eggs and milk until well combined.
3. Add the chopped spinach, crumbled feta cheese, diced red bell pepper, diced onion, chopped fresh herbs, salt, and pepper to the egg mixture. Stir until all the ingredients are evenly distributed.
4. Pour the egg mixture into the prepared muffin tin, filling each cup about 3/4 full.
5. Bake the mini frittatas in the preheated oven for 20-25 minutes, or until they are set and lightly golden brown on top.
6. Once done, remove the mini frittatas from the oven and let them cool in the muffin tin for a few minutes.
7. Carefully remove the mini frittatas from the muffin tin and transfer them to a wire rack to cool completely, or serve them warm.

These spinach and feta mini frittatas are packed with protein, vitamins, and minerals, making them a nutritious and satisfying meal or snack option. They're also great for meal prep and can be stored in the refrigerator for a few days or frozen for longer-term storage. Enjoy these delicious mini frittatas any time of the day!

**Avocado Toast with Radish Slices**

Ingredients:

- 1 ripe avocado
- 2 slices of whole grain bread (or bread of your choice), toasted
- 4-6 radishes, thinly sliced
- Salt and pepper to taste
- Optional toppings: red pepper flakes, microgreens, sliced cucumber, or a squeeze of lemon juice

Instructions:

1. Cut the ripe avocado in half, remove the pit, and scoop the flesh into a bowl.
2. Mash the avocado with a fork until smooth or slightly chunky, depending on your preference.
3. Season the mashed avocado with salt and pepper to taste, and mix well.
4. Toast the slices of whole grain bread until golden brown and crispy.
5. Spread a generous layer of mashed avocado onto each slice of toasted bread.
6. Arrange the thinly sliced radishes on top of the mashed avocado, covering the surface evenly.
7. Optional: Sprinkle red pepper flakes over the radish slices for a hint of heat, or add microgreens, sliced cucumber, or a squeeze of lemon juice for extra flavor and freshness.
8. Serve the avocado toast with radish slices immediately, and enjoy!

This avocado toast with radish slices is a nutritious and satisfying dish that's packed with healthy fats, fiber, and vitamins. It's a great way to start your day or refuel after a workout. Feel free to customize the toppings to suit your taste preferences and get creative with additional additions like sliced tomatoes or a drizzle of balsamic glaze.

**Granola Bars (homemade with oats, nuts, and dried fruit)**

Ingredients:

- 2 cups old-fashioned rolled oats
- 1 cup nuts and seeds (such as almonds, walnuts, pecans, sunflower seeds, or pumpkin seeds), chopped if desired
- 1/2 cup dried fruit (such as raisins, cranberries, apricots, or dates), chopped if large
- 1/4 cup honey or maple syrup
- 1/4 cup nut butter (such as almond butter, peanut butter, or cashew butter)
- 1 tablespoon coconut oil or butter
- 1/2 teaspoon vanilla extract
- Pinch of salt
- Optional add-ins: chocolate chips, coconut flakes, cinnamon, or spices of your choice

Instructions:

1. Preheat your oven to 350°F (175°C). Line an 8x8-inch baking pan with parchment paper, leaving some overhang on the sides for easy removal.
2. In a large mixing bowl, combine the oats, chopped nuts and seeds, and dried fruit. Stir to combine.
3. In a small saucepan, combine the honey or maple syrup, nut butter, coconut oil or butter, vanilla extract, and salt. Heat over low heat, stirring frequently, until the mixture is smooth and well combined.
4. Pour the wet ingredients over the dry ingredients in the mixing bowl. Stir until all the dry ingredients are evenly coated with the wet mixture.
5. If using, stir in any optional add-ins such as chocolate chips, coconut flakes, cinnamon, or spices of your choice.
6. Transfer the mixture to the prepared baking pan. Use a spatula or your hands to press the mixture firmly and evenly into the pan.
7. Bake in the preheated oven for 20-25 minutes, or until the edges are golden brown.
8. Remove the pan from the oven and let the granola bars cool completely in the pan.
9. Once cooled, use the parchment paper overhang to lift the granola bars out of the pan. Place them on a cutting board and use a sharp knife to cut them into bars or squares.

10. Store the homemade granola bars in an airtight container at room temperature for up to one week, or in the refrigerator for longer storage.

These homemade granola bars are nutritious, delicious, and perfect for snacking on the go. Feel free to customize the recipe with your favorite nuts, seeds, dried fruits, and other add-ins to create your own signature flavor combination. Enjoy!

**Roasted Seaweed Snacks**

Ingredients:

- 1 package of dried seaweed sheets (nori)
- 1 tablespoon sesame oil
- Soy sauce or tamari (optional)
- Salt or seasoning of your choice (such as garlic powder, onion powder, or chili flakes)

Instructions:

1. Preheat your oven to 250°F (120°C).
2. Lay the dried seaweed sheets flat on a baking sheet lined with parchment paper or a silicone baking mat.
3. Lightly brush both sides of the seaweed sheets with sesame oil. You can use a pastry brush or your fingers to evenly distribute the oil.
4. If desired, lightly sprinkle soy sauce or tamari over the seaweed sheets for extra flavor. Be careful not to use too much, as seaweed can quickly become salty.
5. Season the seaweed sheets with salt or your favorite seasoning. You can use garlic powder, onion powder, chili flakes, or any other seasoning you like.
6. Once seasoned, place the baking sheet in the preheated oven and bake the seaweed sheets for about 20-25 minutes, or until they are crispy and dry to the touch. Keep an eye on them to prevent burning.
7. Once done, remove the baking sheet from the oven and let the seaweed sheets cool completely before serving.
8. Once cooled, you can cut the roasted seaweed sheets into smaller pieces or leave them whole for snacking.

These homemade roasted seaweed snacks are crispy, savory, and packed with flavor. They make a delicious and nutritious snack that's perfect for satisfying your cravings for something crunchy. Enjoy them on their own or as a topping for salads, soups, or rice dishes!

**Cottage Cheese with Sliced Peaches**

Ingredients:

- Cottage cheese
- Ripe peaches, sliced
- Honey or maple syrup (optional)
- Chopped nuts (such as almonds, walnuts, or pecans) for garnish (optional)

Instructions:

1. Scoop desired amount of cottage cheese into a serving bowl or plate.
2. Wash the peaches thoroughly, then slice them into thin wedges or cubes.
3. Arrange the sliced peaches on top of the cottage cheese.
4. Drizzle honey or maple syrup over the peaches if you prefer a sweeter taste.
5. Optionally, sprinkle chopped nuts on top for added texture and flavor.
6. Serve immediately and enjoy!

This combination of creamy cottage cheese with juicy, sweet peaches is not only delicious but also provides a good balance of protein, fiber, and vitamins. It's a great option for a quick and satisfying snack, breakfast, or light meal any time of the day. Feel free to customize by adding other fruits or toppings according to your taste preferences!

**Veggie Sushi Rolls**

Ingredients:

- Sushi rice (prepared according to package instructions)
- Nori sheets (seaweed)
- Assorted vegetables (such as cucumber, avocado, carrot, bell pepper, and/or cooked asparagus)
- Optional fillings: tofu, pickled radish, or imitation crab sticks
- Soy sauce, wasabi, and pickled ginger for serving

Instructions:

1. Prepare the sushi rice according to package instructions and let it cool to room temperature.
2. Lay a bamboo sushi mat on a flat surface. Place a sheet of nori shiny side down on the mat.
3. Wet your hands with water to prevent the rice from sticking. Spread a thin layer of sushi rice evenly over the nori sheet, leaving about half an inch of space at the top edge.
4. Arrange your choice of vegetables and optional fillings horizontally across the center of the rice-covered nori sheet.
5. Using the bamboo mat as a guide, tightly roll the nori sheet over the fillings, pressing down gently to shape the roll.
6. Once rolled, use a sharp knife to slice the sushi roll into individual pieces, wiping the knife with a damp cloth between cuts to keep it clean.
7. Repeat the process with the remaining nori sheets and fillings.
8. Serve the veggie sushi rolls with soy sauce, wasabi, and pickled ginger on the side for dipping.

Feel free to get creative with your veggie sushi rolls by experimenting with different combinations of vegetables and fillings. You can also try adding a sprinkle of sesame seeds or drizzling with spicy mayo for extra flavor. Enjoy your homemade veggie sushi rolls as a delicious and healthy meal or snack!

**Pumpkin Seeds (roasted with cinnamon)**

Ingredients:

- Pumpkin seeds (also known as pepitas), cleaned and dried
- Olive oil or melted butter
- Ground cinnamon
- Salt (optional)

Instructions:

1. Preheat your oven to 300°F (150°C).
2. In a bowl, toss the cleaned and dried pumpkin seeds with a small amount of olive oil or melted butter until they are evenly coated.
3. Spread the pumpkin seeds in a single layer on a baking sheet lined with parchment paper or a silicone baking mat.
4. Sprinkle ground cinnamon over the pumpkin seeds, tossing them lightly to ensure even distribution.
5. If desired, sprinkle a pinch of salt over the pumpkin seeds for a sweet-savory flavor contrast.
6. Place the baking sheet in the preheated oven and roast the pumpkin seeds for 20-30 minutes, stirring occasionally, until they are golden brown and crispy.
7. Once roasted, remove the pumpkin seeds from the oven and let them cool completely before serving.
8. Store any leftovers in an airtight container at room temperature for up to a week.

These roasted pumpkin seeds with cinnamon are crunchy, flavorful, and packed with nutrients like protein, fiber, and healthy fats. They make a delicious snack on their own, or you can sprinkle them over salads, soups, or yogurt for added texture and flavor. Enjoy this seasonal treat any time of the year!

**Mini Whole Wheat Bagels with Cream Cheese and Tomato**

Ingredients:

- Mini whole wheat bagels
- Cream cheese
- Tomato, thinly sliced
- Optional toppings: red onion slices, cucumber slices, avocado slices, smoked salmon, or fresh herbs like basil or dill

Instructions:

1. Slice the mini whole wheat bagels in half horizontally using a sharp knife.
2. Toast the bagel halves until golden brown and crispy, if desired.
3. Spread a layer of cream cheese on each toasted bagel half.
4. Top the cream cheese with thinly sliced tomato slices, arranging them evenly over the surface.
5. Optionally, add any other toppings of your choice, such as red onion slices, cucumber slices, avocado slices, smoked salmon, or fresh herbs.
6. Place the other half of the bagel on top to form a sandwich.
7. Serve the mini whole wheat bagels with cream cheese and tomato immediately and enjoy!

These mini whole wheat bagels with cream cheese and tomato are delicious, satisfying, and packed with flavor. They're perfect for a quick breakfast, brunch, or as a tasty snack any time of the day. Feel free to customize them with your favorite toppings to suit your taste preferences!

**Blueberry Oatmeal Cookies**

Ingredients:

- 1 cup all-purpose flour
- 1 teaspoon baking powder
- 1/2 teaspoon baking soda
- 1/2 teaspoon ground cinnamon
- 1/4 teaspoon salt
- 1/2 cup unsalted butter, softened
- 1/2 cup brown sugar, packed
- 1/4 cup granulated sugar
- 1 large egg
- 1 teaspoon vanilla extract
- 1 1/2 cups old-fashioned rolled oats
- 1 cup fresh or frozen blueberries

Instructions:

1. Preheat your oven to 350°F (175°C). Line a baking sheet with parchment paper or lightly grease it.
2. In a medium-sized bowl, whisk together the flour, baking powder, baking soda, cinnamon, and salt. Set aside.
3. In a large mixing bowl, cream together the softened butter, brown sugar, and granulated sugar until light and fluffy.
4. Beat in the egg and vanilla extract until well combined.
5. Gradually add the dry ingredients to the wet ingredients, mixing until just combined.
6. Fold in the rolled oats until evenly distributed throughout the dough.
7. Gently fold in the blueberries, being careful not to crush them.
8. Drop rounded tablespoons of dough onto the prepared baking sheet, spacing them about 2 inches apart.
9. Bake in the preheated oven for 10-12 minutes, or until the edges are golden brown and the centers are set.
10. Allow the cookies to cool on the baking sheet for a few minutes before transferring them to a wire rack to cool completely.

These blueberry oatmeal cookies are soft, chewy, and bursting with juicy blueberries. They're perfect for enjoying as a snack or dessert, and they're a great way to sneak some fruit into your day! Store any leftovers in an airtight container at room temperature for up to several days. Enjoy!

**Ants on a Log (celery sticks with peanut butter and raisins)**

Ingredients:

- Celery stalks
- Peanut butter (or any nut or seed butter)
- Raisins

Instructions:

1. Wash the celery stalks thoroughly under cold water and pat them dry with a paper towel.
2. Cut the celery stalks into manageable lengths, typically about 3-4 inches long.
3. Spread peanut butter (or your chosen nut or seed butter) onto each celery stick, filling the center groove where the celery ribbons are.
4. Place raisins along the peanut butter, pressing them gently so they stick. The raisins represent the "ants" on the log.
5. Repeat the process for each celery stick until you have as many "Ants on a Log" as desired.
6. Serve immediately and enjoy!

These Ants on a Log are not only fun to make but also provide a good balance of protein, fiber, and natural sweetness. They make a great snack for kids and adults alike, whether as an afternoon treat or a quick pick-me-up. Feel free to customize by using different nut or seed butters, or by adding other toppings like shredded coconut or chocolate chips.

**Cherry Tomato and Mozzarella Skewers**

Ingredients:

- Cherry tomatoes
- Fresh mini mozzarella balls (bocconcini or ciliegine)
- Fresh basil leaves
- Balsamic glaze (optional)
- Wooden skewers

Instructions:

1. Rinse the cherry tomatoes and basil leaves under cold water, and pat them dry with a paper towel.
2. Drain any excess liquid from the mozzarella balls.
3. Assemble the skewers by threading one cherry tomato, one mini mozzarella ball, and one basil leaf onto each skewer, repeating the pattern until all ingredients are used.
4. Arrange the assembled skewers on a serving platter or plate.
5. Optional: Drizzle balsamic glaze over the skewers for added flavor and presentation.
6. Serve the cherry tomato and mozzarella skewers immediately as a tasty appetizer or snack.

These skewers are not only visually appealing but also bursting with fresh flavors. They're perfect for parties, gatherings, or as a light and refreshing snack any time of the day. Enjoy the combination of juicy tomatoes, creamy mozzarella, and aromatic basil in each bite!

**Whole Grain Crackers with Tuna Salad**

Ingredients:

- Whole grain crackers
- Canned tuna, drained
- Mayonnaise (or Greek yogurt for a lighter option)
- Dijon mustard
- Lemon juice
- Celery, finely chopped
- Red onion, finely chopped (optional)
- Salt and pepper to taste
- Optional add-ins: chopped pickles, capers, fresh herbs (such as parsley or dill)

Instructions:

1. In a mixing bowl, combine the drained canned tuna, mayonnaise (or Greek yogurt), Dijon mustard, and lemon juice. Start with a small amount of each ingredient and adjust to taste.
2. Add finely chopped celery and red onion (if using) to the tuna mixture. These ingredients add crunch and flavor to the salad.
3. Season the tuna salad with salt and pepper to taste. You can also add any optional add-ins, such as chopped pickles, capers, or fresh herbs, for extra flavor.
4. Stir the tuna salad until all ingredients are well combined.
5. Spoon a dollop of tuna salad onto each whole grain cracker, spreading it evenly.
6. Arrange the topped crackers on a serving platter or plate.
7. Optional: Garnish the tuna salad with additional chopped herbs or a sprinkle of paprika for a pop of color.
8. Serve the whole grain crackers with tuna salad immediately, and enjoy!

These whole grain crackers with tuna salad are a convenient and satisfying snack or light meal that's packed with protein, fiber, and essential nutrients. They're perfect for enjoying on their own or as part of a balanced meal. Feel free to customize the tuna salad with your favorite ingredients and adjust the seasoning to suit your taste preferences!

**Mango Chia Seed Pudding**

Ingredients:

- 1 ripe mango, peeled and diced
- 1/2 cup chia seeds
- 2 cups milk (dairy or non-dairy)
- 1-2 tablespoons honey or maple syrup (optional, depending on sweetness preference)
- 1 teaspoon vanilla extract
- Optional toppings: additional diced mango, sliced almonds, shredded coconut, or fresh berries

Instructions:

1. In a blender or food processor, puree the diced mango until smooth.
2. In a mixing bowl, combine the mango puree, chia seeds, milk, honey or maple syrup (if using), and vanilla extract. Stir well to combine.
3. Cover the bowl and refrigerate the mango chia seed mixture for at least 2 hours, or preferably overnight, to allow the chia seeds to thicken and the flavors to meld.
4. After chilling, give the mixture a good stir to redistribute the chia seeds.
5. Divide the mango chia seed pudding into individual serving bowls or jars.
6. Optionally, top each serving with additional diced mango, sliced almonds, shredded coconut, or fresh berries for added texture and flavor.
7. Serve the mango chia seed pudding chilled and enjoy!

This mango chia seed pudding is creamy, fruity, and packed with fiber, omega-3 fatty acids, and antioxidants. It's a healthy and delicious treat that's perfect for satisfying your sweet cravings while also providing a nutritious boost. Enjoy it for breakfast, as a snack, or as a dessert any time of the day!

**Spinach and Cheese Quesadillas (whole grain tortillas)**

Ingredients:

- Whole grain tortillas
- Fresh spinach leaves
- Shredded cheese (such as cheddar, mozzarella, or Monterey Jack)
- Olive oil or cooking spray

Optional Add-ins:

- Sliced bell peppers
- Diced onions
- Cooked chicken or beans
- Sliced mushrooms
- Diced tomatoes
- Avocado slices
- Salsa or guacamole for dipping

Instructions:

1. Heat a skillet or griddle over medium heat.
2. Lightly brush one side of a whole grain tortilla with olive oil or spray it with cooking spray.
3. Place the tortilla, oil side down, on the skillet or griddle.
4. Sprinkle a layer of shredded cheese over half of the tortilla.
5. Add a handful of fresh spinach leaves on top of the cheese.
6. Optionally, add any other desired fillings, such as sliced bell peppers, diced onions, cooked chicken or beans, sliced mushrooms, or diced tomatoes.
7. Sprinkle another layer of shredded cheese over the fillings.
8. Fold the empty half of the tortilla over the fillings to create a half-moon shape.
9. Cook the quesadilla for 2-3 minutes on each side, or until the tortilla is golden brown and crispy, and the cheese is melted.
10. Repeat the process with the remaining tortillas and fillings.
11. Once cooked, remove the quesadillas from the skillet or griddle and let them cool for a minute before slicing them into wedges.
12. Serve the spinach and cheese quesadillas warm with salsa, guacamole, or your favorite dipping sauce on the side.

These spinach and cheese quesadillas made with whole grain tortillas are a delicious and satisfying meal that's packed with fiber, vitamins, and minerals. They're perfect for a quick lunch, dinner, or snack, and you can customize them with your favorite fillings and toppings. Enjoy!

**Roasted Red Pepper Hummus with Pita Bread**

Ingredients:

- 1 can (15 ounces) chickpeas (garbanzo beans), drained and rinsed
- 1/3 cup tahini (sesame seed paste)
- 1/4 cup extra virgin olive oil
- 1/4 cup lemon juice (about 1-2 lemons)
- 2 cloves garlic, minced
- 1/2 teaspoon ground cumin
- 1/2 teaspoon smoked paprika
- 1/2 teaspoon salt, or to taste
- 1/4 teaspoon black pepper
- 1 large roasted red pepper (from a jar or homemade), drained and patted dry
- 2-4 tablespoons water, as needed for consistency
- Pita bread, cut into wedges, for serving
- Optional garnishes: extra olive oil, smoked paprika, chopped fresh parsley, or toasted pine nuts

Instructions:

1. In a food processor, combine the drained chickpeas, tahini, olive oil, lemon juice, minced garlic, ground cumin, smoked paprika, salt, and black pepper.
2. Add the roasted red pepper to the food processor.
3. Process the ingredients until smooth and creamy, scraping down the sides of the bowl as needed.
4. If the hummus is too thick, add water, 1 tablespoon at a time, until you reach your desired consistency.
5. Taste the hummus and adjust the seasoning if needed, adding more salt, lemon juice, or spices to taste.
6. Transfer the roasted red pepper hummus to a serving bowl.
7. Drizzle a little extra olive oil over the top and sprinkle with smoked paprika, chopped fresh parsley, or toasted pine nuts for garnish, if desired.
8. Serve the roasted red pepper hummus with pita bread wedges for dipping.

This roasted red pepper hummus is creamy, flavorful, and perfect for spreading on pita bread or dipping with fresh vegetables. It's a crowd-pleasing appetizer that's easy to make and sure to impress your guests. Enjoy!

**Zucchini Chips**

Ingredients:

- 2 medium zucchinis
- 2 tablespoons olive oil
- Salt and pepper, to taste
- Optional seasonings: garlic powder, onion powder, paprika, or grated Parmesan cheese

Instructions:

1. Preheat your oven to 225°F (110°C). Line a baking sheet with parchment paper or a silicone baking mat.
2. Wash the zucchinis and pat them dry with a paper towel.
3. Slice the zucchinis into thin rounds, about 1/8 inch thick, using a sharp knife or a mandoline slicer.
4. In a large bowl, toss the zucchini slices with olive oil until they are evenly coated.
5. Arrange the zucchini slices in a single layer on the prepared baking sheet, making sure they don't overlap.
6. Sprinkle the zucchini slices with salt and pepper, and any additional seasonings of your choice, such as garlic powder, onion powder, paprika, or grated Parmesan cheese.
7. Place the baking sheet in the preheated oven and bake the zucchini chips for 2-3 hours, or until they are crisp and golden brown, flipping them halfway through the baking time to ensure even cooking.
8. Once the zucchini chips are done, remove them from the oven and let them cool on the baking sheet for a few minutes before transferring them to a wire rack to cool completely.
9. Serve the zucchini chips immediately as a healthy snack, or store them in an airtight container at room temperature for up to a few days.

These homemade zucchini chips are crispy, flavorful, and perfect for snacking on their own or dipping into your favorite sauces or dips. They're a great way to enjoy the natural goodness of zucchini in a fun and tasty way!

**Pineapple Coconut Energy Bites**

Ingredients:

- 1 cup dried pineapple, chopped
- 1 cup shredded coconut (unsweetened)
- 1/2 cup rolled oats
- 1/4 cup almond butter (or any nut or seed butter)
- 1/4 cup honey or maple syrup
- 1 teaspoon vanilla extract
- Pinch of salt (optional)
- Additional shredded coconut for rolling (optional)

Instructions:

1. In a food processor, combine the dried pineapple, shredded coconut, rolled oats, almond butter, honey or maple syrup, vanilla extract, and a pinch of salt, if using.
2. Pulse the mixture until it starts to come together and forms a sticky dough. You may need to stop and scrape down the sides of the food processor a few times to ensure all ingredients are well combined.
3. Once the mixture is well combined and forms a dough-like consistency, transfer it to a bowl.
4. Using clean hands, roll the mixture into bite-sized balls, about 1 inch in diameter.
5. If desired, roll the energy bites in additional shredded coconut to coat the outsides.
6. Place the energy bites on a baking sheet lined with parchment paper and refrigerate them for at least 30 minutes to firm up.
7. Once firm, transfer the energy bites to an airtight container and store them in the refrigerator for up to a week.

These pineapple coconut energy bites are delicious, portable, and perfect for snacking on the go. They're packed with natural sweetness from the pineapple, healthy fats from the coconut and almond butter, and fiber from the oats. Enjoy them as a quick pick-me-up between meals or as a pre- or post-workout snack!

**Whole Grain Muffins with Mixed Berries**

Ingredients:

- 1 1/2 cups whole wheat flour
- 1/2 cup rolled oats
- 1/2 cup brown sugar (or coconut sugar)
- 2 teaspoons baking powder
- 1/2 teaspoon baking soda
- 1/4 teaspoon salt
- 1 cup mixed berries (such as blueberries, raspberries, and chopped strawberries)
- 1/2 cup plain yogurt (Greek yogurt or dairy-free yogurt)
- 1/2 cup milk (dairy or plant-based)
- 1/4 cup unsweetened applesauce
- 1 large egg
- 1 teaspoon vanilla extract
- Optional: 1 tablespoon honey or maple syrup for added sweetness

Instructions:

1. Preheat your oven to 375°F (190°C). Line a muffin tin with paper liners or lightly grease the cups with cooking spray.
2. In a large mixing bowl, whisk together the whole wheat flour, rolled oats, brown sugar, baking powder, baking soda, and salt until well combined.
3. Gently fold the mixed berries into the dry ingredients until evenly distributed.
4. In a separate bowl, whisk together the plain yogurt, milk, applesauce, egg, and vanilla extract until smooth.
5. Pour the wet ingredients into the dry ingredients and stir until just combined. Be careful not to overmix; a few lumps are okay.
6. If desired, stir in honey or maple syrup for added sweetness.
7. Spoon the muffin batter into the prepared muffin tin, filling each cup about 2/3 full.
8. Bake in the preheated oven for 18-20 minutes, or until the muffins are golden brown and a toothpick inserted into the center comes out clean.
9. Remove the muffins from the oven and let them cool in the muffin tin for a few minutes before transferring them to a wire rack to cool completely.

These whole grain muffins with mixed berries are moist, tender, and bursting with fruity flavors. They're a healthier alternative to traditional muffins and are perfect for enjoying any time of the day. Store any leftovers in an airtight container at room temperature for up to several days, or freeze them for longer storage. Enjoy!